AF350840
Learn to
HULA
with Lani
Marcy Schaaf

Table of Content

Aloha,

Welcome to the magical islands of Hawaii, where the sun kisses the ocean, and the palm trees sway with the breeze. In this book, you will join young Lani on an enchanting journey to learn the art of hula, a traditional Hawaiian dance that tells beautiful stories through graceful movements.

Hula is more than just a dance; it's a way to share love, respect, and the vibrant culture of Hawaii. With each step and gesture, hula dancers bring legends, nature, and emotions to life. In "Learn to HULA with Lani," you will discover the meanings behind each hula movement and learn how to dance with your heart.

So, put on your dancing feet, and let's begin our adventure with Lani and her wise grandmother, Tutu. Together, we'll explore the joy and spirit of hula, step by step.

Aloha and enjoy the dance!

Author Bio: Marcy Schaaf

Marcy Schaaf is an internationally acclaimed children's book author celebrated for her unique ability to bring real-life events and current topics into the world of young readers. From exploring the future of technology—like using AI to plan the perfect vacation—to empowering stories about being non-binary, autism, and the art of conversation mapping, Marcy's work is both timely and transformative.

A true global citizen, Marcy has traveled the world, drawing inspiration from the vibrant culture of Grenada, the breathtaking beauty of Hawaii, and the timeless charm of Italy, where she now calls home. Her works resonate with readers from all corners of the globe, and her storytelling reflects the richness of these diverse experiences.

Marcy's innovative voice has not only earned her a loyal readership but also established her as a literary force with a mission to engage young minds in the complexities of our world. Her ability to make topics like social media influence and inclusion accessible and exciting for kids has made her a household name.

And her exclusive Members ONLY Program that gives fans access to brand-new stories not available in retail markets, behind-the-scenes content, and insights into her creative process. Members can choose from 15 languages, receive monthly book shipments, and unlock special content designed exclusively for them. This program also includes members-only events that are by invitation worldwide and a private message from the author on your birthday.

With a heart for storytelling and a passion for inspiring the next generation, Marcy Schaaf continues to push boundaries, one unforgettable book at a time.

On a sunny island
in Hawaii, young
Lani wanted to
learn the hula.

She asked her grandmother,
"Tutu, can you teach me the
hula dance?"

"Of course, Lani!" Tutu said.
"Hula tells beautiful
stories."

"First, we begin with the 'kaholo.' It's a side-to-side step."

"The 'kaholo' step represents the flowing ocean waves."

Lani practiced her 'kaholo' step, imagining the waves.

"Next, we learn the 'ami,' a circular hip movement," said Tutu.

"The 'ami' symbolizes the rolling hills of Hawaii."

Lani's hips moved in circles
like the hills.

"Now, the 'uwehe,' lifting one foot, then the other," Tutu instructed.

"The 'uwehe' shows joy and excitement."

Lani's feet danced with joy,
just like the 'uwehe.'

"Finally, the 'hela,' stepping forward and back," said Tutu.

"The 'hela' represents balance and connection."

Lani practiced the 'hela, feeling balanced and connected.

"Each movement has a special meaning," Tutu explained.

"Hula isn't just dancing; it's telling a story."

Lani danced the
'kaholo,' 'ami,' 'uwehe,'
and 'hela.'

She felt the waves, hills, joy,
and balance.

Lani learned that hula is
more than just dance.

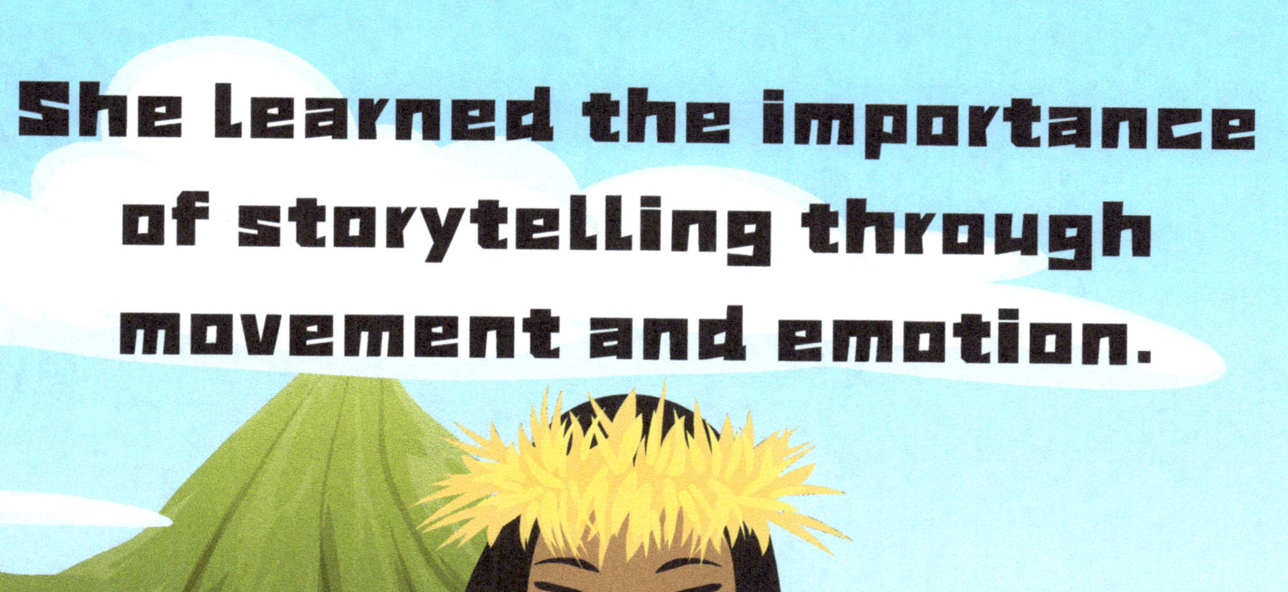

She learned the importance of storytelling through movement and emotion.

"Hula is a gift," Tutu said,
handed down from one
generation to the next,

Lani's heart was full of aloha
for hula.

She danced hula every day with the spirit of Aloha that can only be found in Hawaii!

THE END

Hawaiian Words and Their Meanings

Tutu
Meaning: Grandmother
Explanation: In Hawaiian culture, "Tutu" is a term of endearment and respect for a grandmother. It signifies the wisdom and nurturing nature of elders.

Kaholo
Meaning: A basic hula step
Explanation: The "kaholo" is a fundamental hula movement involving a side-to-side step. It represents the flowing movement of the ocean waves, reflecting the natural beauty of Hawaii.

Ami
Meaning: Circular hip movement
Explanation: The "ami" involves moving the hips in a circular motion. This movement symbolizes the rolling hills and the continuity of nature in Hawaii.

Uwehe
Meaning: Lifting one foot, then the other
Explanation: The "uwehe" is a joyful hula movement where the dancer lifts each foot alternately. It expresses excitement and happiness, bringing a sense of liveliness to the dance.

Hela
Meaning: Stepping forward and back
Explanation: The "hela" involves stepping forward and then back. It symbolizes balance and connection, important aspects of hula that show the dancer's harmony with the earth and surroundings.

Aloha
Meaning: Love, respect, hello, goodbye
Explanation: "Aloha" is a versatile and deeply meaningful word in Hawaiian. It encapsulates love, peace, compassion, and a spirit of kindness. It is used both as a greeting and a farewell, embodying the essence of Hawaiian hospitality and warmth.
Additional Context

Hula: Hula is a traditional Hawaiian dance that tells stories through graceful movements and gestures. Each movement in hula has a specific meaning, often related to nature, emotions, and Hawaiian mythology.
Hawaiian Culture: The culture is rich with traditions and values that emphasize respect for nature, community, and family. Learning and performing hula is one way to pass on these values and keep the culture alive.

THE GIFT SHOP

Embark of your next adventure

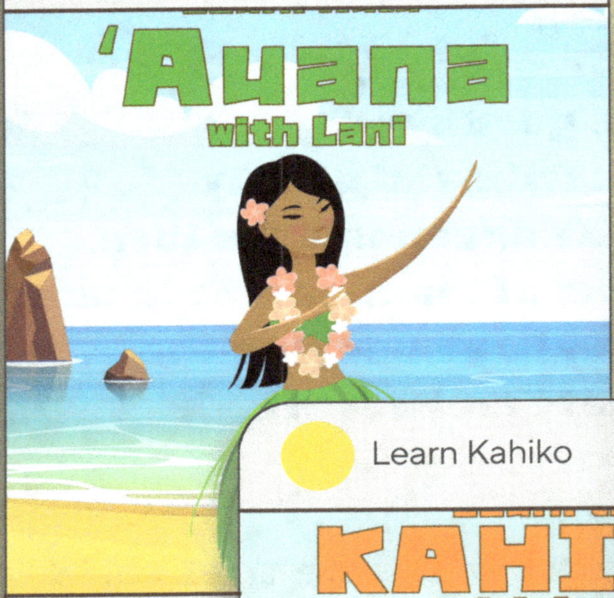

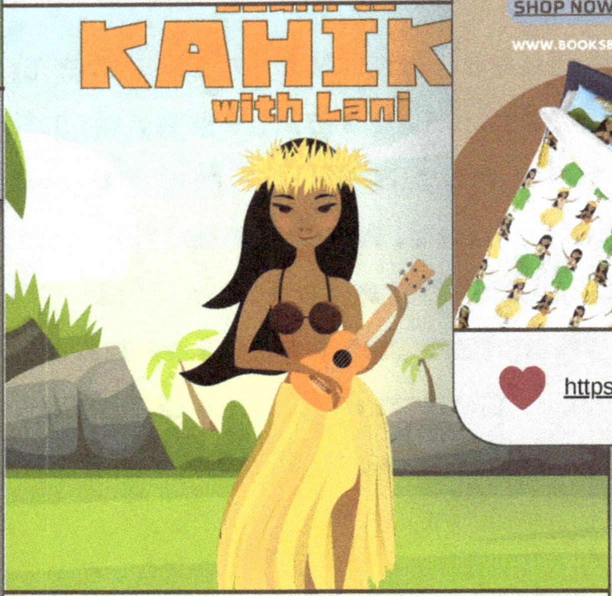

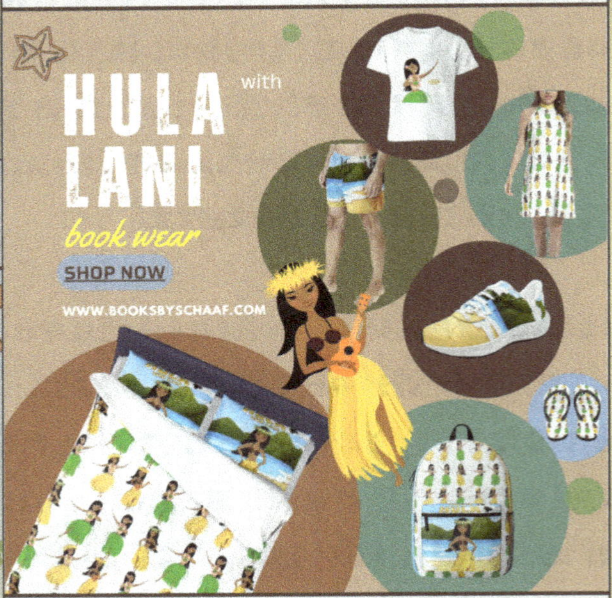

THE GIFT SHOP

Embark of your next adventure

QR Partners

Corporate Program

A Simple QR Code That Entertains Families and Pays You!

Families are already scanning QR codes throughout your property.

Now you can turn those moments into engaging children's entertainment and a new revenue stream — without adding work for your team.

What Is the QR Code Program?

We provide a single, branded QR code that gives families instant access to a curated library of children's digital books in multiple languages.

No apps.

No logins.

No staff training.

Guests scan and enjoy — that's it.

Why Hotels & Resorts Participate

- 📱 Immediate entertainment for children
- 🌍 Multilingual content for international guests
- ⭐ Improved family guest satisfaction and reviews
- 💲 Passive revenue with no upfront cost
- 🏛 No inventory, storage, or maintenance

Once the QR code is placed, the program runs automatically.

Ideal Placement Locations

- Guest rooms
- Pool and lounge areas
- Kids clubs
- Gift shops
- Breakfast and waiting areas

Anywhere families naturally pause.

How Guests Use It

1. Scan the QR code
2. Pick Language
3. Instantly access to children's book
4. One free book every month!

Everything works directly in the browser — no APP to download.

Revenue for Your Property

Every purchase made through your hotel's unique QR code is tracked and shared.

- Your property receives 30% of all guest purchases
- No setup fees
- No monthly costs
- No financial risk

If guests choose to purchase, you earn.

If they don't, there is no cost to you.

Why This Works for Hotels

This program functions like a digital children's amenity:

- Always available
- Always updated
- No physical wear or loss
- No staff involvement

It enhances the guest experience while quietly generating income.

Easy to Test, Easy to Expand

We offer:

- Pilot programs
- Single-location trials
- Multi-property rollout options

Each QR code is uniquely tracked, so performance and revenue remain transparent.

Let's Partner

If your property serves families or international travelers, this program is a natural fit.

to sign up https://payhip.com/BooksBySchaaf/contact

Join Our
Books By Schaaf
AFFILIATE PROGRAM
$
EARN COMMISSIONS!
GET YOUR UNIQUE LINK
SHARE AMAZING BOOKS
Promote Kids' Books & Earn Money!
Easy $$$
Share & Promote
Inspire Young Readers

Affiliate Program
Join the Books By Schaaf Affiliate Team!
Love children's books, language learning, and inspiring young readers around the world? Now you can earn while sharing stories that matter. As a Books By Schaaf Affiliate, you'll earn commission every time someone purchases through your unique link. It's simple, fun, and rewarding!
✅ Why Join?
📚 Promote 500+ engaging children's books
🌍 Support bilingual & multicultural learning
💰 Earn commission on every sale
🎯 No inventory. No upfront costs. No tech skills needed.
Perfect for:
Parents & teachers
Bloggers & influencers
School groups
Travel & hospitality partners
Anyone who loves helping kids learn
💡 How It Works
Sign up as an affiliate
Get your personal link
Share it online, in emails, or in person
Earn commissions when people buy
That's it!
❤️ Make an Impact While You Earn
Every book you share helps children:
✔ Build confidence
✔ Learn new languages
✔ Discover the joy of reading
Join today and become part of a global reading movement.
👉 Sign up now and start earning!

Books By Schaaf

www.BookBySchaaf.com

Bilingual kids books

Paperback, eBooks and Audio

10 minute behind the scenes Podcast on Spotify

Songs exclusively on Audio version

Some books have companion coloring books